考研英语写作
定量分析与定性预测

张纪元　编著

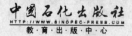

中国石化出版社
HTTP://WWW.SINOPEC-PRESS.COM
教·育·出·版·中·心

图书在版编目（CIP）数据

考研英语写作定量分析与定性预测/张纪元编著.
—北京：中国石化出版社，2007
ISBN 978-7-80229-450-9

Ⅰ.考… Ⅱ.张… Ⅲ.英语-写作-研究生-
入学考试-自学参考资料 Ⅳ.H315.

中国版本图书馆 CIP 数据核字（2007）第 161642 号

中国石化出版社出版发行

地址：北京市东城区安定门外大街 58 号
邮编：100011　电话：(010)84271850
读者服务部电话：(010)84289974
http://www.sinopec-press.com
E-mail：press@ sinopec.com.cn

金圣才文化发展(北京)有限公司排版
北京宏伟双华印刷有限公司印刷
全国各地新华书店经销

*
787×1092 毫米 32 开本 4 印张 64 千字
2008 年 10 月第 2 版　2008 年 10 月第 2 次印刷
定价：12.00 元
（购买时请认明封面防伪标识）

迦思佑® **图书策划委员会**

序　言

目前市面上能看得见的考研写作书籍大致有三类：1）历年真题范文；2）写作模版，即开头句、过渡词、结尾句等固定套路，跟考题并无实质关系；3）定量的押题，如2009年十大热点社会问题等。这三类写作书籍存在以下几点问题：1）历年真题范文缺乏预测性；2）写作模版太虚无，不切题，可能会得零分；3）定量的押题危险性太大，无科学根据，靠的是运气。

本书是定性的预测性书籍，具有以下特点：1）具有很强的科学预测性；2）切题性强，实质内容多；3）包容性强，打破了定量押题的局限性；4）背诵内容少，考生负担小。

为证实这本预测性小书可能具有的巨大实用价值，我把"迦思佑2007年和2008年考研英语写作押题班"及其本书命中的考研英语写作相关内容在这里进行诠释。

一、命中2007年考研英语写作诠释

1. 笔者判断题型：人生哲理。

2. 考试方向：自信。

3. 写作思路：自信是一个人走向成功的主要因素。可举"有志者事竟成"（Nothing is impossible

to a willing heart.）的例子——像爱迪生那样，遇到困难或挫折要有自信，要乐观。

4. 笔者推荐背诵范文："迦思佑2007年考研英语写作押题班讲义"最后一页（2006年12月22日的补充教材）。

5. 使用方法：把变量"perseverance"改为变量"self-confidence"。

人生哲理背诵文本：

From this picture, we can pick up/acquire/obtain/gain/get/secure/chalk up a philosophic theory in life in surprise, which, although there are all sorts of/a number of controversial factors to contribute to success, such as courage and resources, prudence and determination, diligence and frugality, a positive and aggressive attitude, initiative and self-confidence, enthusiasm and optimism, learnedness and curiosity, frustration and perseverance, favorable circumstances, adverse circumstances, and so on, in my view, as this picture indicates, perseverance is one that is often more important than all the others.（85字）

Thomas Henry Huxley, a noted/famous/eminent/well-known/distinguished scientist won the Nobel Prize in 1963, once wrote, "All truth, in the long run, is only common sense clarified."

We <u>might/may/just</u> as well see one <u>typical/representative/well-known/classical</u> example. ......

It is interesting that almost everything is easy to say and difficult to do. Our oldest enemy happens to be ourselves. He/she pesters us all the time just like ghost. When we are determined to perform a worthwhile blueprint, he/she always tells you: "Let it be! Uncalled – for!!" Nonetheless, I am deeply confident that whatever man has done man may do. (60 字)

Support your view with examples:

冰冻三尺，非一日之寒(Rome was not built in one day.)/滴水穿石(Drops of water outwear the stone.)/凡事要有始有终 (Never do things by halves.)/有志者事竟成(Nothing is impossible to a willing heart.): After thousands of efforts to make the electric light bulb produced no illumination, Thomas Edison said, "I haven't failed, I've identified 10,000 ways that it doesn't work." During his lifetime, Thomas Edison invented 1093 different devices including the electric bulb and battery. A number of other great achievers, such as Marie Curie, James Watt, Henry Bessemer, Louis Pasteur, Beethoven, and so on, found that success arrives for everyone who <u>perseveres</u> forever.

经验乃成功之母（Experience/failure is the mother of wisdom/success.）：Thomas Edison's <u>success</u>/wisdom testifies to <u>success</u>/wisdom is really built on the foundations of innumerable <u>failures</u>/experiences.

勤奋近乎成功（Diligence/painstaking work is near success.）：Genius is 1 percent inspiration and 99 percent perspiration. We have electric light bulbs because Thomas Edison refused to give up even after 10,000 failed experiments. Edison usually worked eighteen hours each day, even on every weekend as well as.

顺境与逆境（Favorable Circumstances and Adverse Circumstances）：As <u>Mengzi</u>/Mencius, a great philosopher in china, put it, "When Heaven is about to place a great responsibility on a great man, it always first frustrates his spirit and will, exhausts his muscles and bones, exposes him to starvation and poverty, harasses him by troubles and setbacks so as to stimulate his spirit, toughen his nature and enhance his abilities."

二、命中 2008 年考研英语写作诠释

1. 笔者判断题型：人生哲理（成功的关键因素）。

4

2. 考试方向：合作是成功的关键因素。

3. 写作思路：

1）合作是成功的众多因素中的关键因素之一。

2）小到个人的成功，大到民族的发展或全球问题的解决，合作都是极其重要的。

4. 笔者推荐背诵文本：

1）迦思佑 2008 年《考研英语写作定量分析与定性预测》第 9 ~ 10 页、第 18 ~ 19 页、第 84 页。

2）迦思佑 2008 年"考研英语写作押题班讲义（补充材料）"第 2 页、第 9 页。

5. 相关图片：

迦思佑 2008 年《考研英语写作定量分析与定性预测》

迦思佑 2008 年《考研英语写作定量分析与定性预测》

迦思佑 2008 年《考研英语写作定量分析与定性预测》

6. 本书曾为 2008 年考研英语写作提供的范文：

From this picture, we can pick up/acquire/obtain/gain/get/secure/chalk up a philosophic theory in life in surprise, which, although there are all sorts of/a number of controversial factors to contribute to success, such as courage and resources, prudence and determination, diligence and frugality, a positive and aggressive attitude, initiative and self-confidence, enthusiasm and optimism, learnedness and curiosity, frustration and perseverance, favorable circumstances, adverse circumstances, and so on, in my view, as this picture indicates, perseverance is one that is often more important than all the others. (85 字)

One of the characteristics/properties/features/

virtues/qulities/characters of successful people/notable figures/famous people is having perseverance. For example, Albert Einstein was a simple man but a great scientist in the 20th century, who won a 1921 Nobel Prize. His creativity or scientific accomplishment is the result of a combination of hard work and perseverance.

文化交流(Cultural exchange):

we should extract the essence and abandon the dross from the Western culture.

全球化(Globalization):

With the rapid increase of globalization, our world becomes more and more like a small village, people in global village have much more communication and cooperation by various means than all of the past time and peoples need to understand each other more eagerly than the past.

社会问题重点词汇:

cooperation

气候变暖(Climate change):

Recent decades we have witnessed an obvious rise in the global average temperature, which receives serious concerns across the world. Climate was a global issue and urged all countries to work together to address the issue. The relevant international community should increase financial input and information sharing and step up cooperation in research, development and innovation of technology. We also called on other countries to join hands in dealing with climate change and promoting harmonious, clean and sustainable development in the world.

7. 使用方法：把变量"perseverance"改为变量"cooperation"。

8. 试卷写作内容(建议)：

第一段：描述图片(略)。

第二段：In my view, it is the real meaning of the drawing that cooperation is critical for everyone to achieve the eventual goal. Although there are all sorts of factors to contribute to success, such as courage and resources, prudence and determination, a positive and aggressive attitude, initiative and self-confidence, enthusiasm and optimism, frustration and perseverance, team work or cooperation, and so on, as this drawing indicates, cooperation is one that is usually more important than all the others. (78 字)

第三段：One of the characteristics of successful people is having cooperation. For example, the accomplishment of Bill Gates or Microsoft Corporation is the result of a combination of hard work by himself and team work. In addition, a lot of global problems also need all the country to join hands in dealing with them. For instance, Climate change was a global issue and urged all countries to work together to address the issue. The relevant international community should increase information sharing and step up cooperation in research, development and innovation of technology. (91字)

　　写作是 2009 年硕士研究生入学英语考试中 30 分的考题,几乎占到了总分的三分之一,所以写作部分得分的高低直接关系到整个英语考试的成败。若读者对本书有何疑问或对于本书的修订有何建议,请在迦思佑官方网站(www. jsy. org. cn)上的《张纪元信箱》栏目给笔者写信,笔者将公开回复各位读者的问题。

张纪元
2008 年 10 月 8 日于北京

内容介绍及使用说明

本书对全国硕士研究生入学英语考试的历年写作真题进行了科学性地分析，并建立了一个预测理论体系。本书的主要目的是预测 2009 年硕士研究生入学英语考试的写作考题以及应对策略。

一、关于第一章

这一章对历年真题进行了定量分析并对 2009 年写作考题做出定性预测。这一部分是整本书的理论框架，应认真学习和掌握。

二、关于第二章

第二章是建立在第一章的理论体系基础之上所进行的进一步具体预测。针对往年不同题型所要求的写作步骤给出了背诵文本。背诵文本中如 "**In the picture**/photo/drawing/graph/cartoon/set of pictures" 的内容是同义词的替换，目的是让使用者在考场上写出各有千秋的文章，所以只需挑出一个词背诵即可。标有"参考资料篇"的背诵文本不必背诵，重在模仿写作格式。标有"完全背诵篇"的背诵文本必须熟背，是答题的最关键部分。标有"挑选背诵篇"的背诵文本不必全部背诵，只需针对每一个话题挑选重要的句子或关键词背诵即可。

三、关于第三章

第三章是对于小写作的分析及预测背诵文本，内容很少，应该熟背并学会灵活运用。

四、关于第四章

第四章是超越经验主义的预测。在掌握前三章之余再进行学习和背诵。

五、关于第五章

第五章是笔者个人对英文写作实力提高的看法。

六、关于中文释义

本书英文背诵文本中的很多内容没有给出中文释义，目的是为了让使用者尽量摆脱中文表达方式的束缚，直接背诵原版英文。

七、精简背诵文本的步骤

1）认真学习全书内容。
2）把重复句子划分出来。
3）尽量舍弃标有"挑选背诵"项的背诵文本。
4）最终总结出 7～9 页进行熟练背诵。

目 录

第一章　2009 年考研英语写作预测方法论

一、历年真题定性分析

生活在城市还是乡村
　　（1991 年考题类型→"个人偏好"）

父母和孩子之间缺乏沟通
　　（1992 年考题类型→"无形社会问题"）

电视广告
　　（1993 年考题类型→"无形社会问题"）

结交朋友
　　（1994 年考题类型→"个人偏好"）

希望工程
　　（1995 年考题类型→"有形社会问题"）

健康的身体
　　（1996 年考题类型→"个人偏好"）

世界性的吸烟问题
　　（1997 年考题类型→"有形社会问题"）

不必要的承诺
　　（1998 年考题类型→"有形社会问题"）

"生态失衡
　　（1999 年考题类型→"有形社会问题"）

商业捕鱼

    （2000 年考题类型→"有形社会问题"）

奉献爱心

    （2001 年考题类型→"无形社会问题"）

文化交流

    （2002 年考题类型→"无形社会问题"）

温室里的花朵经不起风吹雨打

    （2003 年考题类型→"人生哲理"）

终点又是新起点

    （2004 年考题类型→"人生哲理"）

养老问题

    （2005 年考题类型→"无形社会问题"）

青少年盲目崇拜

    （2006 年考题类型→"无形社会问题"）

自信

    （2007 年考题类型→"人生哲理"）

合作

    （2008 年考题类型→"人生哲理"）

二、历年真题写作题型定义

1）个人偏好。个人偏好指的是利弊参半的问题，如"生活在农村还是城市"各有利弊，利弊要因每个人的不同偏好而判定。

2）有形社会问题。有形社会问题指的是只有依靠政府才能够解决的一些社会问题，如生态失衡、假冒伪劣产品泛滥等社会问题。

3）无形社会问题。无形社会问题指的是通过政府或法律手段无法很好解决的一些社会问题，如养老问题、青少年盲目崇拜等社会问题。

4）人生哲理。人生哲理指的是不同的人生观和价值观，如逆境出人才、自强不息、勇于拼搏等话题。

三、2009 年考研英语写作题型预测

通过以上对历年写作真题的分析，我们可以看出考研写作的题型已经相当固定。"个人偏好"题型截止 1996 年总共考了三次，接下来的 11 年再也没考过。"无形社会问题"题型考了 6 次。"有形社会问题"题型考了 5 次。从 2003 年开始考"人生哲理"题型，截止 2008 年总共考了 4 次，可以说是新题型。综上所述，2009 年的写作应该是围绕着以上四种题型出题。

第二章 2009 年考研英语大写作预测背诵文本

第一节 无形社会问题背诵文本

保留传统并不意味着因循守旧

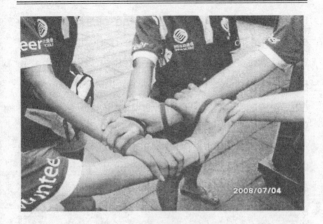

每人都应献出一份力量

一、"无形社会问题"的写作步骤

1. Describe the picture/drawing/photo/graph.

2. Interpret its meaning. / Reasons.

3. Support your view with examples.

4. Give your comments. / Give your point of view.

二、完全背诵篇

1. Interpret its meaning

Obviously/apparently/clearly/undoubtedly/evidently/manifestly/unambiguously/unequivocally, the meaning/message/purpose conveyed/indicated/suggested/implied/hinted by the picture not only show that three sons and one daughter are not willing to maintain their elder father, but, what is more/even more important, that this social problem/phenomenon/issue, which the picture point out, is simply/merely/just/only one of numerous/many/various social phenomena to have become commonplace/ordinary/normal/usual/unexceptional and already attracted broad/great/close/universal/general attention in China in recent years. Over the past quarter of a century/since 1980s/for more than 20 years, China has firmly implemented/enforced/fulfilled/executed/performed the policy of reform and opening up to the outside world, which has brought about/attained/gained/reached/achieved/won rapid economic growth, sustained social progress and continuous betterment/improvement of people's living standard, while China has been experiencing/facing/confronting/undergoing/suffer/encounter a great number of social problems and the collapse/rupture/breakdown/extinguishment/destruction of the invaluable/precious/priceless traditional virtue and culture as well as.

(150 字)

译文：很明显，这幅图画的目的不仅仅是向

6

我们展现三个儿子和一个女儿都不情愿赡养他们的老父亲，而更重要地是告诉我们，图片中指出的这个社会问题仅仅是在最近几年许多已经变得司空见惯，并且引起了广泛关注。在过去的二十多年里，中国已经稳固地实施了改革开放政策，向世界打开国门，并取得了快速的经济增长、持续的社会进步、人们生活水平不断地得到改善，同时中国也一直在经历着各种各样的问题，并且也在遭受着优良传统文化和美德的瓦解。

2. Possible reason for this phenomenon

The reasons for this problem, if the possible ones are enumerated/exemplied/illustrated/instanced/recited one by one/one after another, may be numerous/innumerable/countless. Nevertheless/nonetheless/notwithstanding/however/yet, I believe/feel/consider/deem/reckon/argue/contend/maintain/assert/claim that the main/leading reasons derive from/spring from/arise from/stem from/are due to the social and economic circumstances given. Now China has transformed its planned economy system into an initial socialist market economy system, which has brought about/attained/gained/reached/achieved/won rapid economic growth, sustained social progress and continuous betterment/improvement of people's living standard, while the market economy system is revealing its ugly face, such as energy crisis, environmental pollution and so forth. In a word/in brief/on the whole, there is undoubtedly the reality that Commercialism and westernization erode spiritual values, and degenerate the cultural fabrics of a society. (135 字)

译文：至于这个问题的原因，如果把可能的原因都一一数出来的话，可能是数不清的。尽管如此，我认为主要的原因应归咎于这个特定的社会和经济环境。中国现在已经从计划经济体制转向社会主义市场经济体制，中国已经取得了快速的经济增长、持续的社会进步、人们生活水平不断地得到改善。一句话，如今存在一个不可否认的事实，那就是商业社会和西化影响了精神上的价值观念，同时改变了一个社会的文化结构。

3. Give your comments/Give your point of view

1）用于评论（Comments）

We must first understand the nature of the problem. In my view/in my opinion, On the one hand, It is true that many of China's current/

present/existent/contemporary problems are the inevitable side effects of rapid economic development, which, of necessity, had to occur in an unbalanced way. On the other hand, without the economic development in/about the great number of developing countries or third world countries, like China, there will be no real development, prosperity and stability for the whole country. Notwithstanding/nonetheless/nevertheless/however/ after all, in the long run, Economic development had to come first, but now a more complex agenda of social and political requirements must be integrated and optimized with pure economic growth. So we must promote the coordinated development of material civilization, political civilization and spiritual civilization to build China into a socialist country that is prosperous, powerful, democratic and culturally advanced.

译文：我们必须先要理解这个问题的本质。以我来看，一方面，目前中国存在的许多问题 都是由于别无选择的不平衡的经济快速发展造成的避免不了的负面影响。另一方面，对于大多数像中国这样的发展中国家或第三世界国家来讲，没有了经济的发展，将不存在整个国家的真正的发展、繁荣和稳定。不过，从长远来看，尽管，我们不得不先发展经济，但是如今过多的社会和政治需要必须同纯粹的经济增长结合起来使其最优化。因此，我们必须推动物质文明、政治文明和精神文明协调发展，把我国建设成为富强、民主、文明的社会主义国家。

2) 用于建议(Suggestion)

I have some/several suggestions about this problem. First and foremost/firstly/primarily/mainly/largely/mostly, China should learn from many developed countries/some western countries to dispose of/deal with/handle/solve/settle/iron out this social problem, including other social problems moral and non-moral, by means of/by state legislation, social policy and other relative regulations, especially/particularly because/since China has joined/become a member of the World Trade Organization（WTO）in 2001 and taken place/held the 29th Olympic Games in 2008 as well as. Secondly, our government should clearly/definitely stipulate/establish the responsibilities and obligations of the relative/specific departments for the fulfillment/performance/implementation/execution. Thirdly, in the long run/from a long-term point of view, we should set up/found/constitute/institute a special education system/organization to promote and strengthen/encourage citizens' awareness of environmental protection, and hence improve their values/ideas/notions of consumption and morality. In addition, I recommend that children should start some education of Chinese traditional virtue as early as possible, such as thrift, honesty, affection, filial piety, courtesy, loyalty, humaneness, and so on.

译文：关于这个问题，我有一些建议。首要地，中国应该向众多发达国家学习，通过国家立法、社会政策和其他相关的规章制度来解决这个社会问题，也包括其他的道德的和非道德的社会问题，特别是因为中国已经在 2001 年加入了 WTO，并且中国将在 2008 年举办第 29 界奥运会。其次，更重要的是我们的政府应该清晰地规定相关部门应履行的责任和义务。第三，从长远来看，我们应该设立一个专门的机构去宣传和加强公民对环境保护的意识，从而改变他们的观念。另外，我建议应该尽早地开始对孩子们进行中国传统美德的教育，诸如节俭、诚实、亲情、孝顺、谦恭有礼、忠诚、仁爱等等。

3）用于结尾（Predicting + Conclusion）

In summary, to maintain a sustained, healthy, rapid and coordinated economic development, achieve socialist modernization and a society where man and nature live as friends, and build a harmonious and dynamic society with democracy, rule of law, justice, honesty and decency, stability and order, we will encounter no fewer difficulties and problems, but we are confident in our ability to overcome them and arrive at our set goal triumphantly.

译文：总的来讲，为了维持一个可持续的、健康的、快速的和协调的经济发展，为了达到社会主义现代化和人和自然像朋友一样共生的社会，并且为了建造一个和谐的、有活力的、民主的、法治的、公正的、诚实庄重的、稳固有序的社会，我们肯定会遇到很多困难和问题。但是，我相信我们有能力克服它们，最终会胜利地达到我们的目标。

In summary, China still has a long way to go in this problem and accordingly, great efforts are essential to make in order to solve it. But I am deeply convinced that she, a nation which has civilization for 5,000 years, never loses any good things, physical, intellectual, or moral, till she finds a better substitute, and then the loss is a gain.

译文：总之，中国在这个问题上仍然有一段长路要走，因此为了解决它，我们必须要做出巨大的努力。但是，我深信她，一个拥有 5000 年文明的民族，决不会丢掉任何好的东西，物质的、精神的或道德的，直到她找到一个更好的替代，那么到那时侯这种丢失就是一种获得。

三、挑选背诵篇

Support your view with examples：

1. 文化交流（Cultural exchange）

Now with economic globalization, the Western civilization, especially the American culture, holding the strong position, is exerting its impact on every part of the world, including China. What kind of cultural awareness should we have in copying the Western culture? We daringly take in those that should be taken in and decisively discard those that should be discarded, namely we should extract the essence and abandon the dross from the Western culture. What kind of culture awareness should we have in facing our traditional culture? The traditional Chinese culture, namely Confucianism or the mixture of Confucianism, Buddhism, Taoism and other traditional thinking in ancient China, is a gigantic culture system, which has lasted for over two thousand years. And it has been continuously self-renewing, self-consummating and constantly adjusting itself to the development of the times and society. Not to mention the far-off time, this gigantic culture system, so we should inherit and prosper it.

译文：如今，随着经济的全球化，西方文明，特别是美国文化，夺得了强有力的地位，正在冲击这个世界上的每一部分，包括中国。我们以何种文化意识复制西方文化？我们大胆地吸收那些应该吸收的，果断地抛弃那些该抛弃的，换句话说，我们应取其精华，弃其糟粕。我们以何种文化意识面对我们的传统文化？传统的中国文化，或者说是儒家文化或儒家、佛家和道家文化的混合物，还有其他古代的传统思想，是一个巨大的文化体系，已经持续了二千多年。所以，我们应该继承和发扬。

2. 民族文化 (The ethnic groups)

Culture is a significant character of a nation. It is the soul of a nation that keeps it surviving and going forward; the power that keeps it developing and prospering; and the spring that spouts its energy. China is a united multi-national country. The 56 nationalities jointly created the colorful and profound Chinese culture, in which the ethnic culture composes an important part. The government should pay high attention to the development of the culture cause of the ethnic groups, enact and implement a series of laws and regulations, policies and measures to help the ethnic groups to develop their culture cause from all aspects, which has achieved significant results.

3. 文明冲突(Civilization conflict)

People of **different civilizations**, such as Islamic civilization, Christian civilization or Chinese civilization, have different views on the relations between God and man, the individual and the group, the citizen and the state, parents and children, husband and wife, as well as differing views of the relative importance of rights and responsibilities, liberty and authority, equality and hierarchy. These differences are the product of centuries. They will not soon disappear. They are far more fundamental than differences among political ideologies and political regimes. —— *Harvard University's Samuel Huntington*

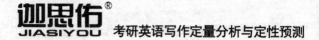

4. 全球化（Globalization）

This is the indication that with the rapid increase of globalization, our world becomes more and more like a small village, people in global village have much more communication and cooperation by various means than all of the past time and peoples need to understand each other more eagerly than the past. Today, cultural and economical globalization has reached almost all nations and regions and the world. Globalization is not only, even mostly not, about the economic reliance on one another, but about the worldshaking change of space and time in our life. Just as US goods flooded world markets in the post-Word War II era, US culture is now penetrating every continent through the dramatic growth of mass communications such as music, television, films and the Internet, as well as through the penetration of American corporations into foreign countries.

5. 互联网（Internet Age）

The arrival of the Internet has speeded up globalization. Currently in China, many Internet cafes, especially those without licenses, admit juveniles in violation of relevant regulations and spread unhealthy information online. They have brought great harm to the mental health of teenagers and interfered with the school teaching, which has aroused strong reaction from the public. **China has the largest population of young netizens in the world, but they turn to the Internet mostly to play games.** The top three activities are online entertainment (39. 9 percent), sports (18. 3 percent) and watching television (12. 3 percent). While blogs, or personal Web logs, have drawn a lot of media attention as a major focus of Internet use, it is clear that young people in particular use the Web for entertainment. Seeking leisure and entertainment has been the primary reason that drives many netizens online, the majority of whom are youngsters. So the issue of China's youth resorting to the Internet for entertainment deserves some attention from our society. The number of China's netizens reached 111 million in 2005, according to the 17th China Internet Development Statistics Report, released in January by the China Internet Network Information Center. And China's cyber-space is dominated by young people. Those between the age of 18 and 24 make up the largest proportion of Internet users, at 35.1 percent. Netizens under the age of 30 account for 71 percent of the total, the report shows. The survey shows that the top five Internet activities are reading news (65.9 percent), browsing Web pages (65.2 percent), playing online games (62.2 percent), downloading music (56.5 percent) and downloading entertainment content (53.5 percent). Internet addiction, mostly resulting from playing online games, is claimed to be the largest problem threatening the healthy growth and development of Chinese youth. **Statistics from the** 2005 **China Youth Internet Addiction Research Report show that** 13.2 **percent of young Chinese netizens suffer from Internet addiction disorder, and another** 13 **percent have the tendency to become addicted to the Internet**. He holds that online entertainment is nothing than Internet "opium", and he calls on young people to abandon their computer screens and get out Internet cafes to seek real entertainment in the real world.

6. 青少年(Young teenagers/young adult/young children)

Since the mid-1990s, there have been about 250,000 suicides every year in China, with suicide ranking as the chief cause of death among people between the ages of 15 and 34. A recent report of the World Health Organization says that over 90 per cent of the suicides in foreign countries suffer from **mental problems**. But in China 37 per cent of the suicides choose killing themselves as a way to **escape daily pressure or disappointments**. A recent case of suicide by **a boy** addicted to Internet games has increased the public's concern over the issue of **Internet Addiction Disorder** (IAD). Xiao Yi, a 13-year-old from Tianjin, committed suicide thinking that he would meet his friends from cyber space after he died. He jumped from the top of a 24-storey high-rise, Beijing Youth Daily reported yesterday. He left four notes before he committed suicide. In the letters Xiao, playing the role of a character from a computer game, said that he wanted to meet three friends who also played the game in paradise. He did not even mention his parents in the letters. In the hypothetical world created by such games, they become confident and gain satisfaction, which they cannot get in the real world, he said. Shen Qiyun, a professor at Beijing Normal University, who has studied the influence on teenagers of such games since 2001, said that currently 80 percent of computer games are imported from abroad, half of which are related to a "demon world", martial arts and violence, which are not healthy influences on teenagers. The country has strengthened its supervision and management of computer games. Increasing stress, loneliness and a lack of medical support for depression are thought to have contributed to an annual suicide toll that is estimated at 250,000 people a year. According to the China Daily, an additional 2.5 million to 3.5 million make unsuccessful attempts to kill themselves each year.

7. 精神空虚(The void spirit)

A lot of people who commit suicide are result from their void spirit. there is a spiritual void in China. Establish and implement the scientific view of development and push forward the coordinated development between socialist material civilization, political civilization and spiritual civilization.

8. 传统美德(Traditional virtue)

For decades, we have made more criticism than inheritance of our own traditional culture and more negative than confirmative. We should certainly learn from the West, but it is of equal importance that we retain virtues of our own. The Confucian Tradition(The Three Essential Confucian Values: I. Filial Piety II. Humaneness III. Respect for Ritual)

9. 铺张浪费(Extravagance and waste)/**勤俭节约**(Industry and economy)

The Chinese government, therefore, is promoting the concept of a thrifty society and frugal economy as a matter of urgency. Chinese laws and regulations concerning energy conservation currently in operation leave a lot to be desired.

第二节　国际层面社会问题
背诵文本

谁来拯救地球？

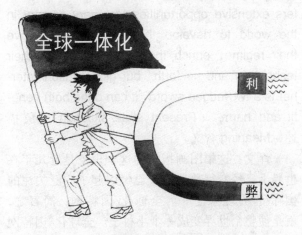

全球一体化

利

弊

如何看待全球化的利与弊?

1. Globalization and Internet

The drawing vividly unfolds ⋯⋯⋯⋯（Describe the picture 描述图画）

This phenomenon which this picture points out is one of numerous international phenomena to have become common and already attracted broad attention in the world in recent years. Globalization/Internet, in brief, makes the whole world a small village. Globalization/Internet offers extensive opportunities for every country in the world to develop their economy, improve their regime, enrich their culture, update their technology and so forth, but globalization/Internet is a two-edged sword: it can bring both benefit and harm. (Present state/situation 现象描述 + Meaning 含义)

译文：这幅图画指出的这个现象是近几年在世界上已经变得普遍并且已经引起了广泛关注的国际/世界现象之一。全球化/因特网，简言之，就是使整个世界变成一个小村子。全球化/因特网给予了这个世界上的每一个国家广泛的机会去发展它们的经济、改善它们的政体、丰富它们的文化、更新它们的技术等等，但全球化/因特网是一把双刃剑：既有利的一面，也有害的一面。

We must first understand the nature of the problem. On the one hand, globalization/Internet offers extensive opportunities for every country in the world. On the other hand, One of the most controversial aspects of globalization/Internet is the global spread and dominance of American culture.

译文：我们必须先要理解这个问题的本质。一方面，全球化/因特网为这个世界上的每一个国家提供了广阔的机会。另一方面，全球化/因特网最具有争议的其中一个方面是认为全球化就是美国文化的全球扩张和一统天下。

I have some suggestions about dealing with this problem. First and foremost, Globalization/Internet can bring benefit. In the past twenty years, in the process of globalization and explosive development of the Internet, China has brought about rapid economic growth, sustained social progress and continuous betterment of people's living standard, so we should accept. Secondly, it can also bring harm. China has been experiencing the collapse of own traditional virtue in the process.

In summary, I am deeply convinced that she, a nation which has civilization for 5,000 years, never loses any good things, physical, intellectual, or moral, till she finds a better substitute, and then the loss is a gain. (Suggestion + conclusion 建议＋结束语)

译文：关于处理这个问题，我有一些建议。首要地，全球化/因特网能带来利益。在过去二十年，在全球化和因特网爆炸性的发展的过程中，中国已经实现了快速的经济增长、持续的社会进步和人们生活水平的不断改善，因此我们是应该接受的。其次，它也能带来伤害，在全球化和因特网爆炸性的发展的过程中，中国一直在经历着自己传统美德的瓦解。

总之，我深信她，一个拥有5000年文明的民族，决不会丢掉任何好的东西，物质的、精神的或道德的，直到她找到一个更好的替代，那么到那时侯这种丢失就是一种获得。

2. 气候变暖(Climate change)

Recent decades we have witnessed an obvious rise in the global average temperature, which receives serious concerns across the world. Climate is a global issue and urges all countries to work together to address the issue. We should pursue economic growth, social development and environmental protection in a coordinated and balanced way, and develop models of production and consumption compatible with sustainable development. The relevant international community should increase financial input and information sharing and step up cooperation in research, development and innovation of technology. Adaptation to climate change is of the greatest concerns to developing countries.

Developing countries should take some policy measures to mitigate greenhouse gas emissions. As a developing country, China will shoulder its due international responsibilities and obligations. The Chinese government should give prominence to building a resource-conserving, environment-friendly society in its strategy of industrialization and modernization. Wen also called on other countries to join hands in dealing with climate change and promoting harmonious, clean and sustainable development in the world.

Hackers' criminal activities are an international problem and China's network and information system have often been attacked by hackers from other countries.

第三节　有形社会问题背诵文本

销毁假冒伪劣产品

一、"有形社会问题"的写作步骤

1. Describe the picture/drawing/photo/graph/ cartoon.

2. Interpret its meaning/message/purpose. /Reasons.

3. Give a specific example.

4. Give your suggestion.

二、参考资料篇

Describe the picture/drawing/photo/graph/cartoon:

The cartoon symbolically states the ways that three sons and a daughter treat their old, helpless father. They each stand in a different corner of a football field. The eldest son kicks out the father, who huddles up into a ball. The other children prepare to ward him off. It is sad to see none of the children is willing to receive their father.

1. In the picture/photo/drawing/graph/cartoon/ set of pictures, we can see/observe/conclude/examine that an old father, like a football, is being kicked out by his oldest son, and rest of his children, the second one, the third one and the youngest one among all, his daughter, all have been refusing to give entry into their house, which in this picture is painted as the four differ-

ent goal posts.

2. The picture **reflects**/depicts a story/tells us that……

3. It is **clearly**/vividly/apparently/obviously **depicted**/showed/drew in the **picture**/photo/drawing/graph that……

4. The little plant, **on the left picture**, is protected under a greenhouse which regulates the supply of energy demanded and protects it from unfavorable weather conditions, **and** once it, **in the right picture**, is kept in the open without any cover, the plant is vulnerable to the unfavorable weather conditions such as rain-fall thunder or hurricane, and hence its flowers may fade and its leaves will wither away sooner than the expected life.

5. The big graph, **on the left**, **represents**/illustrates/depicts the **trend**/tendency/current **that** between 1980 and 1990, the US population has grown to 250 million, **while**/whereas/though the small graph, **on the right**, **represents**/illustrates/depicts **that** the wildlife in population in the US has decreased to 33 million.

6. **The picture on the left** is at an energy

31

where the electrons are trapped between the two atoms of the dimer pair, and all you see is a sort of lozenge or oval. The picture on the right is at an energy where the electrons can sit on one atom or the other, but not in the middle, and you can now see two features in each dimer, corresponding to the two atoms in the dimer pair.

三、完全背诵篇

1. Interpret its meaning/message/purpose

1） Obviously/apparently/clearly/undoubtedly/ evidently/manifestly/unambiguously/unequivocally, the meaning/message/purpose conveyed/indicated/suggested/implied/hinted by the picture not only show that……, but, what is more/even more important, that this social problem/phenomenon/issue, which the picture points out, is simply/merely/just/only one of numerous/many/various social phenomena to have become commonplace/ordinary/normal/usual/unexceptional and already attracted broad/great/close/universal/general attention in China in recent years, such as energy crisis, environmental pollution and so forth. In a word/in brief/on the whole, over the past quarter of a century/since 1980s/for more than 20 years,

China has firmly implemented/enforced/fulfilled/
executed/performed the policy of reform and opening up to the outside world, which has brought a-
bout/attained/gained/reached/achieved/won rapid
economic growth, sustained social progress and
continuous betterment/improvement of people's
living standard, while China has been experien-
cing/facing/confronting/undergoing/suffering/encou-
ntering a variety of/a number of/a series of problems and challenges. (140 字)

　　译文：很明显，这幅图画的目的不仅仅是向
我们展现……，更重要地是告诉我们，图片中指
出的这个社会问题在中国最近几年已经变得司空
见惯，并且引起了广泛关注，诸如能源危机、环
境污染等等。一句话，在过去的二十多年里，中
国已经稳固地实施了改革开放政策，向世界打开
国门，中国已经取得了快速的经济增长、持续的
社会进步、人们生活水平不断地得到改善，同时
中国也一直在经历着各种各样的问题和挑战。

　　2) The meaning/message/purpose of the picture is not so much that it shows that counterfeit
drugs kill the lives of human beings and counterfeit fertilizer and insecticide damage the crops,
but that it hints/indicates/suggests/implies that ……

译文：这幅图画的目的更多地是在暗示我们……，而不单单是展现给我们这样一个画面……

2. Possible reason for this phenomenon

1）The reasons for this problem, if the possible ones are enumerated/exemplified/illustrated/instanced/recited one by one/one after another, may be numerous/innumerable/countless. Nevertheless/nonetheless/notwithstanding/however/yet, I believe/feel/consider/deem/reckon/argue/contend/maintain/assert/claim that the main/leading reasons derive from/spring from/arise from/stem from/are due to the social and economic circumstances given. Now China has transformed its planned economy system into an initial socialist market economy system, which has brought about/attained/gained/reached/achieved/won rapid economic growth, sustained social progress and continuous betterment/improvement of people's living standard, while the market economy system is revealing its ugly face, such as energy crisis, environmental pollution and so forth. Nowadays, in china Mammonism prevails everywhere, and some people who don't have the means to get rich through proper channels resort to cheating, compromising their conscience, counterfeiting and other unethical means towards the goal of personal prosperity. （152 字）

译文：至于这个问题的原因，如果把可能的原因都一一数出来的话，可能是数不清的。尽管如此，我认为主要的原因应归咎于这个特定的社会和经济环境。现在的中国已经从计划经济体制转向了一个初级的社会主义市场经济体制，中国已经取得了快速的经济增长、持续的社会进步、人们生活水平不断地得到改善，然而，市场经济体制的负面影响正在凸现，诸如能源危机、环境污染等等。

2）Generally/largely/chiefly/mainly/mostly/principally the social problem, in my view, resulted from/derived from/sprang from/arose from/stemmed from two reasons. Firstly, since China has transformed its planned economy system into an initial socialist market economy system, the market economy system is revealing its ugly face, such as……Nowadays, some people who don't have the means to get rich through proper channels resort to cheating, compromising their conscience, counterfeiting and other unethical means towards the goal of personal prosperity. Secondly, we are suffering a shortage of legal instruments to penalize such illegalities, and our punishment is too weak to be effective.

译文：在我看来，这个社会问题大致起源于两个原因，第一，因为中国已经从计划经济体制转向了一个初级的社会主义市场经济体制，所以，负面影响正在凸现，诸如…… 第二，我们正在面临一个立法工具对于惩罚这种违法行为成效微弱的局面。

3. Give your suggestion

1）用于建议（Suggestion）

I have some/several suggestions about this problem. First and foremost/firstly/primarily/mainly/largely/mostly, China should learn from many developed countries/some western countries to dispose of/deal with/handle/solve/settle/iron out this social problem, including other social problems moral and non-moral, by means of/by state legislation, social policy and other relative regulations, especially/particularly because/since China has joined/become a member of the World Trade Organization（WTO）in 2001 and will take place/

<u>hold</u> the 29th Olympic Games in 2008 as well as. Secondly, our government should clearly/definitely <u>stipulate/establish</u> the responsibilities and obligations of the <u>relative/specific</u> departments for the <u>fulfillment/performance/implementation/execution</u>. Thirdly, <u>in the long run/from a long-term point of view</u>, we should <u>set up/found/constitute/institute</u> a special education <u>system/organization</u> to promote and <u>strengthen/encourage</u> citizens' awareness of environmental protection, and hence improve their <u>values/ideas/notions</u> of consumption and morality. In addition, the <u>huge/massive/large task/project/work</u> depends on <u>conscientious/active</u> participation and support by every Chinese citizen as well as. (145 字)

译文: 关于这个问题, 我有一些建议。首要地, 中国应该向众多发达国家学习, 通过国家立法、社会政策和其他相关的规章制度来解决这个社会问题, 也包括其他的道德的和非道德的社会问题, 特别是因为中国已经在 2001 年加入了WTO, 并且中国将在 2008 年举办第 29 界奥运会。其次, 更重要的是我们的政府应该清晰地规定相关部门应履行的责任和义务。第三, 从长远来看, 我们应该设立一个专门的机构去宣传和加强公民对环境保护的意识, 从而改变他们的观念。另外,

这个问题也需要每一个中国公民的尽心尽责的参与与支持。

2）用于评论（Comments）

We must first understand the nature of the problem. In my view, On the one hand, It is true that many of China's current problems, such as …… and so forth, are the inevitable side effects of rapid economic development. On the other hand, without the economic development in/about the great number of developing countries like China, there will be no real development, prosperity and stability for the whole country. Notwithstanding/nonetheless/nevertheless/however/after all, in the long run, economic development had to come first, but now a more complex agenda of social requirements must be integrated and optimized with pure economic growth. So we must promote the coordinated development of material civilization, political civilization and spiritual civilization to build China into a socialist country that is prosperous, powerful, democratic and culturally advanced.

译文：我们必须先要理解这个问题的本质。以我来看，一方面，目前中国存在的许多问题，

诸如 …… 等等，都是由于经济快速发展造成负面影响。另一方面，对于大多数像中国这样的发展中国家来讲，没有了经济的发展，将不存在整个国家的真正的发展、繁荣和稳定。不过，从长远来看，尽管，我们不得不先发展经济，但是如今过多的社会需要必须同纯粹的经济增长结合起来使其最优化。因此，我们必须推动物质文明、政治文明和精神文明协调发展，把我国建设成为富强、民主、文明的社会主义国家。

3）用于预测（Prediction）

In summary, China still has a long way to go in this problem and accordingly, great efforts are essential to make in order to solve it. We will encounter no fewer difficulties and problems as we stride ahead, and there are bound to be new challenges. But we are confident in our ability to overcome them and arrive at our set goal triumphantly.

译文：总的来讲，中国仍然有很长的路要走，因此为了解决这个问题必须做出极大的努力。当我们向前迈进的时候，我们将会面临很多困难，并且一定存在很多新的挑战，但我相信，我们有能力克服他们，最终胜利地达到我们的目标。

四、挑选背诵篇

Give a specific example:

1. 资源保护(Energy and Resource Saving)

China energy crisis has become a serious problem, which will prevent the rapid development of China economy. For instance, the status of decreasing of the stockpile of national fossil fuel, such as petroleum, natural gas and coal, and increasing of the consumption demand makes it very urgent to find some measures to resolve this crisis. Exploiting some alternative, especially renewable and clear energy resources such as hydrogen energy, wind energy, solar energy and nuclear energy will be the main way to resolve the crisis. Besides, energy-saving and international cooperation in energy field are also another two important channels to alleviate this problem.

译文:中国的能源危机已经成为非常严重的一个问题,它将阻碍中国经济的快速发展。例如,国内的天然矿物燃料储存量,如石油、煤、天然气等,一直在减少,而消费需求一直在增加的这种状况使得我们去寻求解决这些危机的一些措施是迫切的。开发一些可替代的,特别是可持续并且清洁的资源,如氢能、风能、太阳能和核能,将是解决危机的主要途径。此外,能源节约和在能源领域的国际合作也是另外两个缓解危机的主要渠道。

2. 环境污染(Enviromental pollution)

We gave high priority to conserving resources and protecting the environment. A large number of backward production facilities were shut down in accordance with the law. They include small thermal power plants with a total capacity of 21.57 million KW, 11,200 small coal mines, backward iron smelting facilities with a total capacity of 46.59 million tons, backward steel plants with a total capacity of 37.47 million tons and cement plants with a total capacity of 87 million tons. Ten major energy-saving projects were launched. Breakthroughs were made in carrying out desulfurizing projects for coal-fired power plants. The central government provided financial support for 691 projects to prevent and control water pollution in major river valleys. Work continued on ecological conservation projects such as those to protect natural forests and control the factors causing sandstorms in Beijing and Tianjin. During the five-year period, the area of farmland retired for forestation and other lands planted with trees amounted to 31. 91 million hectares, and grazing land returned to natural grasslands totaled 34. 6 million hectares. Protection of land and water resources was strengthened, with a total of 1. 526 million hectares of farmland being upgraded, reclaimed or newly developed over the last five years. In 2007 there was a 3. 27% year-on-year drop in energy consumption per unit of GDP, and for the first time in recent years there was a reduction in both chemical oxygen demand and the total emission of sulfur dioxide, with the former down 3. 14% and the latter down 4. 66% from the previous year. People became more aware of the importance of conserving resources and protecting the environment and made greater efforts in this area. Substantial progress was made in infrastructure development and ecological and environmental conservation projects, and development of key areas and industries with local advantages was accelerated.

—— *from Report on the Work of the Government* (2008) *delivered by Premier Wen Jiabao at the First Session of the* 11th *National People's Congress on March* 5, 2008

3. 环境保护(Environmental protection)

Environmental investment is gradually becoming a critical factor for the implementation of environmental policy, research and development of environmental technology, solution of outstanding environmental problems, improvement in overall environmental quality, and achievement of sustainable development. China faces "grave" soil pollution that jeopardizes the ecology, food safety, people's health and the sustainable development of agriculture, according to the State Environmental Protection Administration (SEPA). China should introduce advanced coal-burning/energy and resource saving technologies that would help increase energy efficiency and protect the environment.

译文：在环境保护方面的资金投入逐渐地成为关键的因素，对于环境政策的实施、环境保护技术的研究和开发、突出的环境问题的解决、整体环境质量的改善和可持续发展的实现来说。中国面临着严重的土壤污染，土壤的严重污染危机到生态、健康的食物、人们的身体健康和农业的可持续发展，根据国家土地保护管理局报道。中国应该引进先进的煤的燃烧技术，这些技术将有助于增加能源的效率，并且也能保护环境。

43

4. 人口增长（The growth of China's population）

With the growth of China's population, the development of the economy and the continuous improvement of the people's consumption level since the 1970s, the pressure on resources, which were already in rather short supply, and on the fragile environment has become greater and greater. The overpopulation has already seriously endangered to **the national survival and the development**/the national economy and the people's livelihood.

译文：自从20世纪70年代，随着中国人口的增长、经济的发展和人们消费水平的不断改善，中国在已经相当短缺的资源供应和脆弱的环境方面的压力开始变得越来越大。过多的人口已经严重威胁到国计民生。

5. 生态失衡（The global ecological imbalance）

The well being of humanity and all life depends on a healthy environment and the balance of local and global ecological systems that support and sustain life. Human activity has created an imbalance in these ecosystems, and we are using up vital resources faster than nature can replace them. Forests are disappearing, deserts are expanding, water tables are dropping, fish populations are diminishing and Earth, water, and air are being contaminated with toxins and greenhouse gases. By burning vast quantities of oil and coal that have been stored under the surface of the earth during millions of years, the carbon dioxide released into the air prevents the sun's heat from radiating back out into space (the greenhouse effect). The automobile leaves a much larger "ecological footprint" than the bicycle. The resultant global warming and climate change present one of the greatest threats to human health and life in the near future. It is urgent that the knowledge and technology exist for reducing the rate of global warming, minimizing toxic waste, replacing use of fossil fuels with healthy and renewable sources of energy, protecting forests and fisheries, and reestablishing a health-sustaining ecological balance, worldwide. However, those who set the agenda for the global economy give higher priority to short-term economic growth than to sustainable human and environmental health.

译文：森林在消失，沙漠在扩张，地下水位

在下降，鱼类的数量在降低，地球、水和空气在被毒素和温室气体玷污。在降低地球变暖的速度，使有毒工业废物最小化，用健康可持续的能源替代天然的矿物燃料，保护生态和鱼类，在全世界重建一个健康可持续的生态平衡等方面的知识产生是迫切需要的。

6. 非法的毒品交易 (The unlawful traffic in drugs)

According to data published by the United Nations in 2005, 81 million people worldwide suffered from cocaine or heroin addiction. The majority of drug users are under 30 and approximately 30 percent are heroin or cocaine addicts. Increasing of the population on drugs is directly connected with the illegal transaction of drugs. What are the physical, social and economic consequences of heroin addiction? Heroin users often experience extreme deterioration of health. They are at high risk for infections, HIV, the virus that causes AIDS, Hepatitis B and C, sexually transmitted diseases, and tuberculosis. If financial resources are insufficient to support the addiction, family and housing stability may be threatened and criminal activity as a means of support may arise accordingly.

译文：按照联合国在 2005 年发布的数据，全世界 8100 万人对可卡因和海洛因上瘾。吸毒人口的增加直接和毒品的非法交易相关联。吸食海洛因造成的身体、社会和经济后果是什么？吸食海洛因的人通常在遭受着健康的不断恶化。他们很容易患传染病、艾滋病、B 和 C 型肝炎、性传播疾病和结核病。如果资金来源不足的话，家庭可能会分裂，犯罪活动将会相应地产生。

7. 艾滋病(HIV/AIDS)

China had 840,000 HIV/Aids patients at the end of 2003, according to official data, but it is believed that the actual figure is much higher.

译文：据官方统计，中国在 2003 年底已有 84 万艾滋病感染者，但是大家普遍认为，实际人数肯定更高。

8. 刺激品(Stimulus)

Coffee, tea, alcohol, sleeping pills, tobacco and chocolate anything that can change our moods, feelings or behavior should be considered a drug. Heavy drinking, as we know, can damage the liver, brain, stomach and other organs. Heavy smoking damages the lungs and heart. Many drugs, like heroin, alcohol and co-caine, can be fatal at high doses.

译文：咖啡、茶、酒精、安眠药、烟草和巧克力等任何能改变我们情绪、感情和行为的物品都应该被认为是一种药物。正如我们所知，大量的饮酒会毁坏肝脏、大脑、胃和其他身体器官。大量的抽烟毁坏了肺和心脏。诸如大量的服用海洛因、酒精和可卡因等许多药物可能是致命的。

9. 家庭问题(The Problem of Domestic or Family Violence)

Under the new style of living where both parents are working, children are not able to get there rightful share of parental love as a result of which the understanding between child and his/her parents is not enough which even some times leads to harsh treatment of children by their own parents. The second type of domestic violence could be the fight between husband and wife which in different societies like India may involve the sister-in-laws and the mother-in-laws, and which results into beating up of the wife by the family members. Over 85 percent of reported victims of domestic violence are women and most perpetrators are men. The children turn to the streets due to family neglect, parents' divorce, and domestic violence. **One of the greatest challenges facing the domestic violence movement is the widespread perception that spousal abuse is a "private matter".** Going forward, Mrs Yu-Foo stressed the need to raise public awareness on domestic violence and offer support to victims. In particular, the Singapore—an government (like many governments around the world) is keen to engage the private sector in helping to tackle this difficult task. **To raise money to support women and children affected by domestic violence. Most Chinese provinces, municipalities and autonomous regions have enacted laws and regulations to curb and prevent domestic violence.** Family violence is no longer considered a domestic affair. **Frequency of parental violence against children in Chinese families**: Impact of age and gender. Domestic violence, regarded traditionally as a private affair to be kept in the family, is increasingly becoming a target of protest and government action. In traditional Chinese culture, men play the dominant role in public and private life, with women expected to be subordinate. "Social acquiescence and tolerance of domestic violence are partly a result of this mentality," said Hou Zhiming, director of the Maple Women's Psychological Counseling Centre, which was founded in 1988. "It is imperative that an anti-domestic violence network be set up, led by governments with the participation of women's federations, law enforcement organs and communities," Hou said. In March, the All-China Women's Federation and Mary Kay Cosmetics jointly launched a women's rights protection hotline (12338) and still another anti-domestic violence hotline (16838198). A legal aid centre for women was also established by the federation, providing regular legal services and psychological counseling. Domestic violence includes physical, sexual and psychological abuse, and more than 90 per cent of victims are women, said Wang Xingjuan, 75, a noted researcher in this field. A national law covering domestic violence is urgently needed, according to Xia Yinlan from the China University of Politics and Law. However, there are many obstacles in the way of building a complete legal system to protect women and children. In the absence of regulations, nongovernmental organizations have played an important role in preventing domestic violence.

10. 就业问题(The laid-off staff and workers)

The central government should establish the unemployment benefit system/a social assistance system to provide basic living allowances and re-employment subsidies to employees laid off from state-owned enterprises. The central government should set up reemployment programs to assist laid-off workers to receive the training they need. Laid-Off Workers also must strengthen own study in order to found a new work to realize re-employment.

译文：中央政府应该设立一个社会援助体系，为那些从国有企业下岗的职工提供基本的生活补贴和再就业补贴。中央政府应该制订再就业方案去帮助下岗职工接受他们需要的培训。下岗职工也必须加强自己的学习，以便找到一个新的工作，实现再就业。

11. 社会保障问题(Social security fund)

The deterioration in economic and social security has largely emerged with the rapid socioeconomic transition and social reconstruction including mass migration. I recommend that there is a need to develop social policy which is specifically focused on a comprehensive lowest living security system. **The establishment of social insurance fund system may cause these unemployed to draw the lowest living expense, the Minimum Living Standard Scheme (MLSS) or dibao, to safeguard social stability.**

12. 假冒伪劣产品问题 (Counterfeits and unqualified products)

These manufacturers, which have sneaked into the market due to slack government control, fail to meet the national quality standard. They must be closed to prevent rampant counterfeits and unqualified products from going on sale to the public.

13. 消费者权益保护问题 (The protection of consumers' rights and interests)

China will strive to establish a perfect system for protecting consumers' rights in the 21st century, which is based on legislative protection, and guaranteed by administrative, judicial and social protection, said Gan Guoping, deputy director of the State Administration for Industry and Commerce. The latest international experiences and practices in the protection of consumers' rights and interests shall be absorbed and taken for reference. Second, **it is necessary to strengthen market supervision and management, and to refine gradually the administrative system for the protection of consumers' rights and interests.** It is essential to establish a perfect consumer complaining and reporting service network with telephone No. 12315 to provide timely solutions to consumption-related disputes and seriously investigate and deal with cases of infringement on consumers' rights and interests; focused on crackdown on the illegal activities of manufacturing and selling fake and shoddy commodities, it is necessary to continue efforts in this regard in key areas and trades and concerning major commodities. Third, it is imperative to mobilize various social forces and give full play to the role of the social system for protecting consumers' rights and interests, it is necessary to accelerate the establishment of a social protective system featuring consumers' organization of self-aid, trade association, enterprise self-discipline, news media and public supervision.

译文：我们必须加强对于市场的监管，逐步地完善消费者权益保护的行政体系也是必须的。

14. 知识产权保护问题 (Intellectual property protection)

The intellectual property protection system emerged as a product of the development of human civilization and commodity economy and, in various countries, it has increasingly become an effective legal tool for protecting the interests of the owner of intellectual products, promoting the development of science, technology and the social economy, and allowing international competition. It is urgent to establish a relatively comprehensive and perfect legal system, such as the Trademark Law and the Copyright Law, for the protection of intellectual property rights, in order to protect the interests of the owner of intellectual products and promote the development of science, technology and the social economy. China has a glorious tradition of innovation that is greatly hampered by today's IP [intellectual property] environment. U. S. officials believe that ineffective protection of intellectual property rights (IPR) hurts both countries. Domestic innovators and investors will be discouraged from developing new products if their hard work is likely to be stolen by IPR thieves. **Piracy in China is rampant and negatively affects everything from computer software and medicine to clothing, auto parts and chewing gum.** It affects both Chinese and foreign IPR holders, and is a growing concern for major trading partners such as the United States and the European Union. At the national level, the Chinese government has taken some positive steps to comply with global IPR requirements, especially since the country's 2001 accession to the World Trade Organization (WTO). **According to the OECD, lack of IP protection might eventually reduce foreign direct investment (FDI) in China as multinationals become wary of transferring sophisticated technology or trade secrets.**

译文：为了保护知识产权，为了保护知识产品拥有者的利益，为了促进科学技术和社会经济的发展，建立一个相对比较全面和完善的法律体系是迫切需要的。

第四节　人生哲理背诵文本

怎样才能步入成功之门？

中华民族传统美德

一、"人生哲理"的写作步骤(Directions)

1. Describe the picture/drawing/photo.

2. Interpret its meaning. / Point ·· its implications in our life.

3. Support your view with exampl

二、完全背诵篇

1. 成功的关键因素(Critical Suc

In my opinion, it is the real/in

deniable/uncontrovertible/unequivocal/

sure-enough meaning of the drawing

ance is critical for everyone to achi

tual goal. Although there are all so

_of_ controversial factors to contribut

such as courage and resources,

determination, diligence and fruga

and aggressive attitude, initiative

dence, enthusiasm and optimism

and curiosity, frustration and perseverance, favorable circumstances, adverse circumstances, cooperation, chance or opportunity, destiny or fortune, and so on, in my view, as this picture indicates, perseverance is one that is usually more important than all the others. (93字)

It is interesting that almost everything is easy to say and difficult to do. Our oldest enemy happens to be ourselves. He/she pesters us all the time just like ghost. When we are determined to perform a worthwhile blueprint, he/she always tells you: " Let it be! Uncalled – for! !" Nonetheless, I am deeply confident that whatever man has done man may do. (60 字)

Support your view with examples:

冰冻三尺，非一日之寒(Rome was not built in one day.)/ 滴水穿石(Drops of water outwear the stone.)/凡事要有始有终 (Never do things by halves.)/ 有志者事竟成(Nothing is impossible to a willing heart.) :

After thousands of efforts to make the electric light bulb produced no illumination, Thomas Edison said, "I haven't failed, I've identified 10,000 ways that it doesn't work. " During his lifetime, Thomas Edison invented 1093 different devices including the electric bulb and battery. A number of other great achievers, such as Marie Curie, James Watt, Henry Bessemer, Louis Pasteur, Beethoven, and so on, found that success arrives for everyone who perseveres forever.

经验乃成功之母（Experience/failure is the mother of wisdom/success.）：

Thomas Edison's success/wisdom testifies to success/wisdom is really built on the foundations of innumerable failures/experiences.

勤奋近乎成功（Diligence/painstaking work is near success.）：

Genius is 1 percent inspiration and 99 percent perspiration. We have electric light bulbs because Thomas Edison refused to give up even after 10,000 failed experiments. Edison usually worked eighteen hours each day, even on every weekend as well as.

顺境与逆境（Favorable Circumstances and Adverse Circumstances）：

As Mengzi/Mencius, a great philosopher in China, put it, "When Heaven/God is about to assign a great responsibility/mission/lifework/vocation to a person, it always firstly agonizes his spirit, exhausts his muscles and bones, hungers his guts and fatigues his body, and disturbs his all intents, so that he/she has the heart to do everything to improve/enhance/heighten/intensify his abilities."

59

译文: 故天将降大任于斯人也,必先苦其心志,劳其筋骨,饿其体肤,空乏其身,行拂乱其所为,所以动心忍性,曾益其所不能。

It would be easier for people with unlimited passion to succeed or achieve their goals than those without passion.

One of the characteristics/properties/features/virtues/qulities/characters of successful people/notable figures/famous people is having perseverance, including novelists, engineers, scholars, poets, artists, thinkers, writers, and mathematicians. For example, Albert Einstein was a simple man but a great scientist in the 20th century, who won a 1921 Nobel Prize. Albert Einstein had a great effect on science and history, and his achievement was even greater than only a few other great scientists have achieved. His creativity or scientific accomplishment is the result of a combination of hard work and perseverance. (82字) In addition, A number of great scientists found that success favors those who persevere, such as Edison Thomas Alva, Alfred Nobel, Sir Isaac Newton, Albert Einstein, Marie Curie,

Huxley Thomas Henry, James Watt, Henry Bessemer, Louis Pasteur, Beethoven, Qian Xuesen, Mao Yisheng, and so on.

Marie Curie is not only the first woman to be awarded a Nobel Prize, but also one of four persons to have been awarded the Nobel Prize twice.

Perseverance is one of important qualities which a scientist should have.

To a large extent, perseverance is essential/critical/crucial to achieving success.

It would be easier for people with unlimited passion to succeed or achieve their goals than those without passion.

2. 人生观和价值观 (Philosophy of life and values of life) 背诵文本
Explain its intended meaning:

In my view, it is the real/indisputable/undeniable/uncontrovertible/unequivocal/unquestionable/sure-enough meaning of the drawing that we should live each day with gentleness, vigor and a keenness of appreciation, and Life lies in

struggling. Greed is a false value. **Often we go about our petty tasks, hardly aware of our true values of life.** The picture enlightens us becoming more appreciative of the meaning of life and its permanent spiritual values. Life is ten percent what you make it and ninety percent how you take it. The value of life lies not in the length of days, but in the use we make of them. So having right values in life is very important for us, especially youngster. (103 字)

生活有百分之十在于你如何塑造它，有百分之九十在于你如何对待它。生命的价值不在于能活多少天，而在于我们如何使用这些日子。

Support your view with an example/examples：座佑铭(My motto for life)

"The past does not equal the future" Anthony Robbins.

"The best way to predict the future is to create it."

Her personal motto is "Challenges make life interesting, overcoming them makes life meaningful. Enjoy life and believe in yourself".

Wish you an endless view to cheer your eyes? Then one more story mount and higher rise.

译文： 欲穷千里目，更上一层楼。

As an ancient Chinese motto puts it, "As Heaven keeps vigor through movement, a gentleman should unremittingly practice self-improvement."

Life lies not in living but in liking.

译文： 生活的意义并不在于活着，而在于爱好人生。

The important thing in life is to have a great aim, and the determination to attain it.

Only a life lived for others is a life worthwhile.

译文： 只有为别人而活，生命才有价值。

出处： A. Einstein 爱因斯坦

I want to bring out the secrets of nature and apply them for the happiness of man. I don't know of any better service to offer for the short time we are in the world.

译文：我想揭示大自然的秘密，用来造福人类。我认为，在我们的短暂一生中，最好的贡献莫过于此了。

出处：Edison 爱迪生

Living without an aim is like sailing without a compass.

译文：生活没有目标就像航海没有罗盘。

We must accept finite disappointment, but we must never lose infinite hope.

译文：我们必须接受失望，因为它是有限的，但千万不可失去希望，因为它是无穷的。

出处：Martin Luther King. Jr. 马丁·路德·金

A man's life is limited, but there is no limit to serving the people. I will dedicate my limited life to the limitless job of serving the people.

译文：人的生命是有限的，可是，为人民服务是无限的，我要把有限的生命，投入到无限的为人民服务之中去。

出处：Lei Feng 雷锋

I am not afraid of tomorrow for I have seen

yesterday and I love today.

译文: 我不害怕明天,因为我见过昨天,又热爱今天。

出处: W. A. White 怀特(美国记者)

Goals determine what you are going to be.

译文: 目标决定你将成为什么样的人。

出处: Julius Erving 朱利叶斯·欧文

A little of everything, and nothing at all.

译文: 什么都来一点,什么也得不到。

出处: Montaigne 蒙田

Laziness is like a lock, which bolts you out of the storehouse of information and makes you an intellectual starveling.

译文: 懒惰是一把锁,锁住了聪明和智慧的仓库,使你在工作和学习上永远是个"缺粮户"。

Chinese society is undergoing a transition. some people have lost their direction and have blurred the differences between right and wrong, honor and disgrace. The concept is a perfect a-malgamation of traditional Chinese values and modern virtues. I should build up socialist concept of honor, disgrace to study the meaning of the concept and learn how to tell right from wrong, good from evil and beauty from ugliness.

The masses, especially the youth, should maintain socialist morality in line with the Eight Honors and Disgraces:

——Love the country; do it no harm.

译文： 以热爱祖国为荣，以危害祖国为耻。

——Serve the people; never betray them.

译文： 以服务人民为荣，以背离人民为耻。

——Follow science; discard superstition.

译文： 以崇尚科学为荣，以愚昧无知为耻。

——Be diligent; not indolent.

译文： 以辛勤劳动为荣，以好逸恶劳为耻。

——Be united, help each other; make no gains at other's expense.

译文： 以团结互助为荣，以损人利己为耻。

——Be honest and trustworthy; do not sacrifice ethics for profit.

译文： 以诚实守信为荣，以见利忘义为耻。

——Be disciplined and law-abiding; not chaotic and lawless.

译文： 以遵纪守法为荣，以违法乱纪为耻。

——Live plainly, work hard; do not wallow

in luxuries and pleasures.

译文：以艰苦奋斗为荣，以骄奢淫逸为耻。

The concept, which underlines the value of patriotism, hardwork and plain living, belief in science, consciousness of serving the people, solidarity, honesty and credibility, and observation of the law, aims to refresh China's values by amalgamating traditional Chinese values with modern virtues.

三、参考资料篇

Charles Nicolle（1866 ~ 1936）：法国细菌学家，他曾因发现斑疹伤寒由体虱传播而获得 1928 年诺贝尔奖

Chance favors only those who court her.

Napoleon Hill（1886 ~ 1977）：英国生理学家，曾获 1922 年诺贝尔生理学 – 医学奖

Every adversity, every failure, every heartache carries with it the seed of an equal or greater benefit.

Henry Ford（1863 ~ 1947）：美国汽车制造商

Failure is only the opportunity to begin again

more intelligently.

H. Jackson Brown Jr.：Opportunity Quote

Nothing is more expensive than a missed opportunity.

Harry Truman(1884～1972)：美国第33任总统(1945～1953年)

A pessimist is one who makes difficulties of his opportunities and an optimist is one who makes opportunities of his difficulties.

Winston Churchill(1874～1965)：英国政治家及作家，(1940～1945)、(1951～1955)两度任首相，1953年诺贝尔文学奖得主

A pessimist sees the difficulty in every opportunity；an optimist sees the opportunity in every difficulty.

Dave Weinbaum：Opportunity Quotes

A window of opportunity won't open itself.

Francis Bacon(1561～1626)：英国哲学家、随笔作家、朝臣、法理学家和政治家

A wise man will make more opportunities

than he finds.

Napoleon Bonaparte(1769 ~ 1821)：法国皇帝
Ability is of little account without opportunity.

Eric Hoffer：Quotations：Opportunity
We are told that talent creates its own opportunities.

Orison Swett Marden：Quote：Opportunity
The golden opportunity you are seeking is in
yourself. It is not in your environment; it is not in
luck or chance, or the help of others; it is in
yourself alone.

Unknown Author：Quote：Opportunity
The impossible is often untried.

Nick Saban：Quotes about Chance
What happened yesterday is history. What
happens tomorrow is a mystery. What we do today makes a difference—the precious present
moment.

Alexander Graham Bell(1847 ~ 1922)：苏格

兰裔美籍电话发明者

When one door closes another door opens；but we so often look so long and so regretfully upon the closed door, that we do not see the ones which open for us.

Author unknown：Quotes about Opportunity

Some people not only expect opportunity to knock, they expect it to beat down the door.

Benjamin Disraeli（1804 ~ 1881）：英国政治家，曾任首相（1868 年和 1874 ~ 1880 年）

The secret of success in life is for a man to be ready for his opportunity when it comes.

Louis Pasteur：Quotes：Opportunity

Luck favors the mind that is prepared.

Benjamin Disraeli（1804 ~ 1881）：英国政治家，曾任首相（1868 年和 1874 ~ 1880 年）

Through perseverance many people win success out of what seemed destined to be certain failure.

第五节 个人偏好背诵文本

一、"个人偏好"的写作步骤

1. Advantage
2. Disadvantage
3. Disadvantages of both
4. My preference

二、个人偏好部分话题

1. 在大企业工作还是小企业工作?

Just as there are distinct differences between being a small fish in a big pond and a big fish in a small pond, so it is with working as a subordinate in a large enterprise and presiding in a small firm. With the former, you can derive a deep sense of satisfaction from being a member of well-known organizations such as General Motors, or the Bell Telephone System. You have the opportunities of learning from experienced executives and knowing about the standard(a. 第一流的, 标准的) working process. With the latter, you have greater responsibilities and your decision may bring immediate effect. Normally you are exposed to various experiences and expected to do a great many things without much help or guidance. **Personally I prefer to** work in a small enterprise, where my prospect of promotion is more bright as long as I work hard. To tell the truth, I'd rather become a well-known and important figure within my own small pond.

2. 独立居住还是与父母同住?

As to me, I like an independent life style in spite of the fact I love my parents. Different generations have different life styles and values. What one generations likes may not be another generation's fondness. Living separately, each generation can enjoy different value. In addition, by leading an independent life, I can train my character and develop my own ability to deal with things encountered in my life.

三、个人偏好背诵文本

The drawing vividly unfolds that ……. Obviously, this question would be answered by everyone in our life, one of the most disputable and controversial questions too.

译文: 很明显,这个问题是我们在生活中都要回答的一个问题,也是最富有争议的问题之一。

Advantage and disadvantage are two sides of the same coin. we should see one side of the advantage while looking at another side of the disadvantage. The answer to this question, in my perspective, may be no absolute, no right or wrong, and depends on different people. On the one hand, the biggest disadvantage is that ⋯⋯. In this case, undoubtedly, It should be totally accepted(denied) by us.

译文：利弊是同一个钱币的两个面，我们在看到利的一面的同时，也要看到不利的一面。以我来看，对于这个问题的回答可能不是绝对的，可能没有对与错之分，它要取决于不同的人。

Nevertheless, on the other hand, in the long run, apparently the vast majority of young/old people consider the disadvantage potential bigger than the advantage, assuming that ⋯⋯ . In terms of this angle, we have to acknowledge that ⋯⋯ is half-and-half of the advantage and the disadvantage.

In summary, to tell the truth, I prefer ⋯⋯ to ⋯⋯ . I think that people's preference are different from each other, and that no amount of getting after them is going to change them. Nor is there any reason to change them, because the differences are probably good, not bad.

译文：说句实话，总的来讲，两者相比，我更喜欢……。我认为，人们的偏好是彼此不同的，并且大多数人们的偏好是很难改变的。不过，也没有任何理由去改变他们，因为这种偏好的不同或许是好的，而不是坏的。

第三章　2009 年考研英语小写作预测背诵文本

一、小写作分析

确切来讲，今年的小作文不具有很强的可预测性。因为只考过四年，所以不存在足够的预测的前提和条件。但通过四年的考试方向来看，都是在直接或间接地围绕在校大学生或刚毕业大学生出题，特别是与自身情况密切相关的话题。所以，笔者建议考生多准备一些与自身有关的材料进行背诵。

二、小写作背诵文本

1. 目的 (Aim)

I am too excited and delighted at your reply. Thank you very much for your speedy and informative reply to my message. I am writing in the hope to recommend myself as a qualified candidate for application of your department's position to further my study in Applied Physics toward Master degree in your university, as advertised on the Linguist list. It is a great honor for me being invited to give this talk today, to celebrate Prof. T. D. Lee's 75th birthday. First of all I must really apologize to you for my inexcusable, inconsiderate behavior, especially the fact that I was not able to post anything. However, I want to let you know that I will be posting next week as usual.

译文： 我对你的回信感到非常的荣幸。由于你们在《语言学家》杂志上登的广告，我正在满怀希望地写这封自荐信来申请攻读你们学院的应用物理学硕士学位。今天我非常荣幸地被邀请做这个讲话来庆祝 Prof. T. D. Lee 的 75 岁生日。首先我对于我的轻率行为向你道歉，特别是我没能邮寄任何东西给你。但是，我希望你知道我下周会照常邮寄给你。

2. 咨询或请求(Asking or Request)

I would like to know if there are any scholarships for international students. I wish to enroll in the Computer Graphics course at London University, and I would like to ask you to write a letter of recommendation. Could you please send me some entrance information about the course of Applied Physics offered at your university? I would be grateful if you could send me the Graduate Application Forms, the Application Forms for Scholarships/Assistantships, a detailed introduction to the School of Physics, and other relevant information. My mailing address is shown on the top of this letter.

译文：我想知道是否有提供给国际学生的奖学金。我想要参加伦敦大学的电脑制图课程，所以，我想请你写一封推荐信。你可以发给我一些你们学校提供的有关应用物理学课程的入学信息吗？如果你能发给我研究生申请表格、奖学金助学金申请表格、一本有关物理学院的详细介绍用书和其他相关的申请资料的话，我将感激不尽。我的邮寄地址显示在这封信的最上方。

3. 个人背景(Personal Background)

I am a 22 year old who grew up in a small town called Brentwood in the East Bay. I was born in Mexico and came to California when I was 4 years old.

译文：我今年 22 岁。在 the East Bay 的一个叫 Brentwood 的小镇上长大。我出生在墨西哥，四岁的时候来到加利福尼亚。

4. 教育(Education)

At the outset, let me introduce myself. My name is Li Ming, and I am currently in my fourth year aiming to get an Honour's Double Major BA in Computer Information Systems and Sociology at the University of Cambridge (U. K.). I am presently in the process of finishing my dissertation at the University of Cambridge (U. K.), and I expect to complete it by April 2006. Furthermore, through four years of hard work, I have gained a vast amount of knowledge concerning my field of major. However, I have recently been considering switching my major to Journalism.

译文: 先让我介绍一下我自己。我叫黎明，我现在在英国剑桥大学读大四，正在为获得计算机信息系统和社会学两个专业合一的学士学位而努力。我正在撰写我的学位论文，并期望能够在2006年4月完成。此外，通过四年的努力学习，我已经获得了大量有关我专业领域的知识。然而我最近一直在考虑把我的专业转到新闻专业上。

5. 成就(Accomplishments/Achievements)

During my undergraduate study, my academic records kept distinguished among the whole department. I was granted First Class Prize every semester, and my overall GPA (89. 5/100) ranked No. 1 among 113 students. Furthermore, most of my theses are awarded Essay of the Year. Last year I took the paper-based TOEFL and got an total score of 650.

译文： 在我的本科学习期间，我的理论课成绩在整个学院里始终都很突出。我每个学期都拿一等奖学金，还有我的 GPA 是 89. 5 分，在 113 个同学中名列第一。此外，我的大多数论文都被评为年度最佳论文。去年我参加了 TOEFL 的笔试，总分考了 650。

6. 经验(Experiences)

In addition, I worked part-time for IBM and Microsoft Corporation as a software testing researcher in the research department, where they offered me the opportunity to apply classroom theory to practice in the workplace and become familiar with their organization, work style and corporate culture.

译文： 我在微软和 IBM 的研究部门做过兼职软件测试员。在那里它们给我提供了一个把课堂理论运用到工作实践中的机会，并且也给我提供了一个熟悉它们的组织结构、工作风格和公司文化的机会。

7. 兴趣(Academic interests and Other interests)：

My academic interests and passions are in social policy and social justice, and I am thinking about social welfare research too. I would like to pursue these passions on a national level and eventually on an international level. And, I would like to start this pursuit while completing my Master and PhD. My hobbies are swimming, reading books, and cooking.

译文：我的学术兴趣和热情在社会政策和社会正义上，并且也一直在思考社会福利研究。我想在国内层面，进而最终在国际层面追求这些酷爱。我想在开始这些追求的同时完成我的硕士和博士学位。我的业余爱好是游泳、读书和烹调。

8. 个性(Character/personality)

I like long-range planning, working by myself, sometimes working on a team, and being the master of my own destiny.

译文：我喜欢做长期打算；独立工作；有时也喜欢团队工作；我喜欢自己掌握自己的命运。

9. 未来目标(Future goals)

Once I graduate from the University of Cambridge, I would like to become a loan officer for a little while. I am an entrepreneur at heart and would like to open up a business of my own. I hope to have a further study and continue to do my research work if I succeed in obtaining the engineering scholarship.

译文：等我在剑桥大学毕业了，我会先做一段时间信贷员。我内心很想成为一个企业家，从而开创自己的事业。我希望能进一步地学习，继续我的研究工作，如果我能成功地获得工程学奖学金的话。

10. 强项或长处(Strengths)

My strengths include creativity and ingenuity, excellent strategizing skills, self-control and self-regulation ability, love of learning, and open-mindedness. My level of knowledge or ability is adequate, but I wish to excel. For me, the five key strengths are ranked as follows: gratitude, optimism, zest, curiosity, ability to love and be loved.

译文：我的强项包括独立创新能力、卓越的策划能力、自我控制和自我调整能力、爱学习、思想开明。我的知识和能力是足够的，但我喜欢超越。下边列出了我的五个强项：感恩、乐观、热情、好奇心、爱与被爱的能力。

11. 弱点(Weaknesses/shortcomings)

As for my weaknesses, I feel that I am prone to take on a very heavy workload, and I stick to my guns about my own work, but I would like to take criticism carefully and a great deal of reflection.

译文：至于我的弱点，我觉得我倾向于承担非常重的工作量，并且我对于我自己的工作固执己见，但我愿意认真地接受别人的批评，并且做出深刻的反思。

12. 感谢语(Acknowledgement)

I just wanted to let you know how much I enjoyed your classes, and I think that your classes will leave a permanent imprint on my heart. Thank you so much for your willingness to share with us your wealth of knowledge. You are the inspiration for my career. Thanks a lot. Thank you for your kind assistance. I really appreciate that you took so much time to acquaint me with the company.

译文：我仅仅想让你知道我是多么地喜欢你的授课，我认为你的讲学将永远留在我的心中。非常感谢你愿意同我们一起分享你的知识财富。你鼓舞着我的一生。非常感谢！谢谢你友好的帮助。

13. 结束语（Ending）

I have asked Professors John Mc Carthy, Robert Gilpin and John Kingston to send you letters of recommendation. The attachment is in Acrobat PDF format, so if you have any problem in opening it, please let me know and I can send you a hard copy. Copies of my certificates and credentials will be sent to you under separate cover（ad. 在另函中）. Please look over the enclosed/attached resume, which provides more details about my background. I will arrange to come in for（v. 接受）an interview at your convenience. I am more than willing to answer any of your questions concerning my application and research. Thank you for your consideration, and I look forward to hearing from you at your earliest convenience. With best wishes for the festive season. I would be grateful if you would send me a graduate catalog of your university and any other necessary information, and also a set of application forms for admission. Would you please send me the application forms for admission and financial support? Thank you again for the opportunity to interview for the marketing position. I appreciated your hospitality and enjoyed meeting you and members of your staff. I look forward to hearing from you to arrange for an interview at your earliest convenience. I look forward, Mr. Weatherby, to hearing from you concerning your hiring decision. Again, thank you for your time and consideration.

第四章 超越经验主义的预测

一、教育问题背诵文本

1. 教育及其教育改革的重要性

It is recognized by everybody that the strength of a country depends upon its education. The higher the education standards, the stronger the country becomes. It should be recognized that our current educational development still cannot fully meet the needs of the social, economic, scientific and technological development. Many Chinese educators, parents and politicians have long been calling for a fundamental reform in the country's education system in order to adapt effectively to the needs of socialistic market economy, globalization and the 21st century.

2. 人文性的教育与实用性的教育

Firstly, practical education should be the central project of the current reform and practice on education. While enjoying a rapidly growing economy for more than 20 years, China has begun to witness an increasing shortage of skilled professionals. To resolve the problem, experts urged more efforts to promote vocational education and shed the outdated practice that only stresses the diploma of higher education. China needs more professionals of certain skill to support its economic growth, and such people can be trained by developing vocational education. Secondly, since the human being came to existence, people began to explore the relationship among the God, nature and human being. Humanism is just the choice from these three. It is also the affirmation to self value and ability. Education, which is a key link in the social development, takes the responsibility to portray human being. To develop humanism has been the trend of the modern development of education.

3. 全球化环境下的课程改革

China's education system should adapt to the market economy and globalization by introducing suitable academic and practical courses from abroad and otherwise changing the education system. Firstly, emphasis on practical course is demanded by our ever-developing society. If a student has little knowledge of computer, English or business, he will lag behind the times. The balance should be tipped toward practical courses in school curriculums. Secondly, as English is greatly emphasized with the rapid development of global communication, correcting the defects that exist in current education system are needed urgently.

二、学者问题背诵文本

1. 学术抱负

My first introduction is to be a student interested in international affairs, especially the economic growth of nations, poverty reduction, and role of leadership in the economic policy making. My research work is a neither purely economic study nor purely political, which is a political economic approach to analyze the growth history of China and India. My second introduction is that I am a student of foreign language. I started learning in 2000, and since then I am trying to speak and write good mandarin. I believe that in order to understand Chinese politics and economy I had to have master the mandarin spoken by 1. 3 billion Chinese and many overseas Chinese in South East Asia and other part of the world.

Through my research work I want to establish a fact that the role of leadership, international environment, and political stability are three major prerequisites of economic growth of a nation. My comparative study of growth in India and china will use the macro policy making process, foreign economic policy, and the role of private and state enterprises as framework to establish the above conclusions.

I aspire to be part of economic policy making in India that will be possible only when I qualify for civil services exam, or become the member of Indian parliament.

2. 学者精神

I think that Chinese scholars should possess the following six spirits. Firstly, as Thomas Edison put it, "Genius is 1 percent inspiration and 99 percent perspiration." Secondly, as Si Maqian noted, "an alp is so steep that you will stop your step when you look it and landscape can not go there as well, and although I'm not capable of mounting it, I want to climb up it in my heart." Thirdly, we should be to ordain conscience for Heaven and Earth, to secure life and fortune for the people, to continue lost teachings for past sages and to establish peace for all future generations. Fourthly, it is our maxim that while I have little possession at hand, I care deeply about my people across the land. Having devoured ten thousand books and drawing inspiration from ancient thinkers, I have the whole world in my mind. Fifthly, it is our selfhood forever that neither riches nor honors can corrupt me, neither poverty nor humbleness can make me deviate from my principle, and neither threats nor forces can subdue me. Sixthly, as Kant said, "there are two things that fill my mind with ever increasing admiration and awe: the starry sky above me and the moral law within me."

译文: 我认为中国的学者应具备以下六种精神: 第一, 正如爱迪生指出的那样, 天才是1%的灵感加上99%的汗水。第二, 如太史公司马迁说:"高山仰止, 景行行止, 虽不能止, 然心向往之。"第三, 我们应该做到为天地立心、为生民立命、为往圣继绝学、为万世开太平。第四，我们的格言应当是这样："身无半亩，心忧天下；读破万卷，神交古人"。第五，"富贵不能淫，贫贱不能移，威武不能屈"将永远是我们的人格。第六，正如康德所说："有两种东西，我对它们的思考越是深沉和持久，它们在我心灵中唤起的惊奇和敬畏就会日新月异，不断增长，这就是我头上的星空与心中的道德定律。"

三、女性问题

宠物（pet）、时尚（fashion）、减肥（slimming/losing weight）、美容与整容（beautifying the face/cosmetic surgery）

Seeking a perfect self is everyone's wish. Nowadays many people try to obtain external beauty by purchasing some expensive clothing and accessories, beautifying their faces, losing weight, and so on. A charming "S" curve stature is a dream of every female, but many improper method of losing weight, such as medication, excessive dieting and overloading exercise, will injure physical healthy, causeing more harm than good.

In my view, we should more run after internal beauty than external beauty because external beauty is less short-lived than internal beauty, and it is not real virtue. I recommend that we had better gradually consummate ourself by reading a number of books, developing a variety of skills, cultivating all kinds of moralities, participating in a great diversity of charitable organizations and so forth.

第五章　英文写作
水平提高浅谈
——复杂思维表达三段论

特别说明：

1）英文写作能力的提高很大程度上是通过模仿优美的原汁原味的英文文章进行培养的。由于本书是预测性的应试书籍，所以没有必要用大量的笔墨讲授如何提高英文写作实力。本章节的目的是引导读者正确地运用有效的方法提高写作能力。写作能力的提高是需要长期培养的，但路径是很快就能掌握的。希望读者能够很好地理解本章的内容，从而掌握一种有效的路径提高自己的英文写作能力。

2）中文书面表达方式和英文书面表达方式存在很大的差异。英文写作能力提高的捷径就是对比中英文表达方式的差异，学会把中文表达方式转换为英文表达方式。

一、主语的几种表达方式

1. 他们能够保存自己历史的唯一途径就是，由讲述人一代接一代地将史实描述为传奇故事口传下来。

The only way that they can preserve their history is to recount it as sagas—legends handed down from one generation of story-tellers to another.

写作法则提炼： 中文表达"他们能够保存自己历史的唯一途径"；英文表达"唯一途径 that 他们能够保存自己的历史"，完全转换"The only way that they can preserve their history"。

2. 弗吉尼亚·伍尔夫(Virginia Woolf)关于她写作《黛洛维夫人》(Mrs. Dalloway)意图的具有争议性的陈述通常被评论家们所忽略了，因为它突出反映了她诸多文学兴趣中某一方面，而这一方面则与人们对"诗性"小说家(poetic novelist)所形成的传统见解大相径庭。所谓的"诗性"小说家，关注的是审视想入非非和白日梦幻的诸般状态，并致力于追寻个体意识的通幽曲径。

Virginia Woolf's provocative statement about her intentions in writing Mrs. Dalloway has regularly been ignored by the critics, since it highlights an aspect of her literary interests very different from the traditional picture of the "poetic" novelist concerned with examining states of reverie and vision and with following the intricate pathways of individual consciousness.

写作法则提炼：中文表达"弗吉尼亚·伍尔夫（Virginia Woolf）关于她写作《黛洛维夫人》（Mrs. Dalloway）意图的具有争议性的陈述"；英文表达"弗吉尼亚·伍尔夫的具有争议性的陈述关于她的目的在写作《黛洛维夫人》"，完全转换"Virginia Woolf's provocative statement about her intentions in writing Mrs. Dalloway"。

3．据估计，在英国，蜘蛛一年里所消灭昆虫的重量将会超过这个国家人口的总重量。

It has been estimated that the weight of all the insects destroyed by spiders in Britain in one year would be greater than the total weight of all the human beings in the country.

写作法则提炼：中文表达"据估计，在英国，蜘蛛一年里所消灭昆虫的重量将会超过这个国家人口的总重量"；英文表达"它已经被估计 that the 重量 of 所有昆虫毁灭的被蜘蛛在英国在一年里将是更大比 the 总重量 of 所有人类在这个国家"，完全转换"It has been estimated that the weight of all the insects destroyed by spiders in Britain in one year would be greater than the total weight of all the human beings in the country"。

4. 企图消除自己和读者之间距离或企图用不了解自己的人的角度来研究自己塑造的形象，很可能会是作家自己毁灭，因为他已经开始为取悦他人而写作了。

This temptation to cover the distance between himself and the reader, to study his image in the sight of those who do not know him, can be his undoing: he has begun to write to please.

写作法则提炼： 中文表达"企图消除自己和读者之间距离或企图用不了解自己的人的角度来研究自己塑造的形象"；英文表达"这种企图去消失距离之间自己和读者，去研究他自己塑造的形象以这种角度 of those who 不了解他自己"，完全转换"This temptation to cover the distance between himself and the reader, to study his image in the sight of those who do not know him"。

二、谓语的几种表达方式

1. 此外，蜘蛛不像其他一些食虫动物，它们绝不会对我们或我们的财物造成丝毫的危害。

Moreover, unlike some of the other insect eaters, spiders never do the least harm to us or our belongings.

写作法则提炼： 中文表达"蜘蛛不像一些其他

食虫动物，它们绝不会对我们或我们的财物造成丝毫的危害"；英文表达"不像一些 of the 其他食虫动物，蜘蛛绝对不做最小的伤害对我们或我们的财物"，完全转换"unlike some of the other insect eaters, spiders never do the least harm to us or our belongings"。

2. 美国的经济体制是围绕着一个以私有企业为主和以市场为导向的经济进行组织的，在这种经济中，消费者很大程度上通过在市场上花钱购买那些他们最想要的商品和服务来决定什么应该被制造。

The American economic system is organized around a basically private-enterprise, market-oriented economy in which consumers largely determine what shall be produced by spending their money in the marketplace for those goods and services that they want most.

写作法则提炼：中文表达"美国的经济体制是围绕着一个以私有企业为主和以市场为导向的经济进行组织的"；英文表达"美国的经济体制被组织围绕一个主要的私营的企业，市场为导向的经济"，完全转换"The American economic system is organized around a basically private-enterprise, market-oriented economy"。

3. 然而，在起初完全不是这么一会事。

In the pioneering days, however, this was not the case at all.

写作法则提炼：中文表达"然而，在起初完全不是这么一会事"；英文表达"在起初，然而，this was 不是这事完全"，完全转换"In the pioneering days, however, this was not the case at all"。

4. 他宣称他反对把这种非同寻常的畜牧繁殖技术用于克隆人类，并下令联邦政府基金不准被用于做此类试验——尽管还没有人建议这么做，而且他还邀请了一个由普林斯顿大学校长哈罗得·夏皮罗所主持的独立专家小组在 90 天内向白宫汇报关于制订有关克隆人的国家政策的建议。

Declaring that he was opposed to using this unusual animal husbandry technique to clone humans, he ordered that federal funds not be used for such an experiment—although no one had proposed to do so, and asked an independent panel of experts chaired by Princeton President Harold Shapiro to report back to the White House in 90 days with recommendations for a national policy on human cloning.

写作法则提炼：中文表达"他宣称……，并下令……, 而且他还邀请……"; 英文表达"宣称 that……, 他下令 that……and 邀请……", 完全转换"Declaring that ……, he ordered that …… and asked ……"。

三、宾语的几种表达方式

1. 我们从书籍中可读到, 5000 年前的近东地区的人们最早学会了写字。

We can read of things that happened 5,000 years ago in the Near East, where people first learned to write.

写作法则提炼: 中文表达"我们从书籍中可读到, 5000 年前的近东地区的人们最早学会了写字"; 英文表达"我们能够读到 things that happened 5000 年前在近东, where 人们最早", 完全转换"We can read of things that happened 5,000 years ago in the Near East, where people first learned to write"。

2. 现在每个人都拥有比任何时代人都要多的可利用信息, 而找到与他/她的特定问题相关的那一点信息的工作不仅复杂、耗时, 有时甚至比登山还难。

The individual now has more information available than any generation, and the task of finding that one piece of information relevant to his or her specific problem is complicated, time—consuming, and sometimes even over-whelming.

写作法则提炼： 中文表达"现在每个人都拥有比任何时代人都要多的可利用信息"；英文表达"个体现在有更多信息可利用的比任何一代人"，完全转换"The individual now has more information available than any generation"。

3. 现代的登山运动员们试图通过一条会给他们带来运动乐趣的路线去攀登山峰，并且这条路线愈艰险愈带劲儿。

Modern alpinists try to climb mountains by a route which will give them good sport, and the more difficult it is, the more highly it is regarded.

写作法则提炼： 中文表达"现代的登山运动员们试图通过一条会给他们带来运动乐趣的路线去攀登山峰，并且这条路线愈艰险愈带劲儿"；英文表达"现代的登山运动员试图去登山通过一条路线 which 将给他们好的运动，并且 the 更多的困难的 it 是，the 更多的兴奋地 it 被认为"，完全转换"Modern alpinists try to climb mountains by a route which will give them good sport, and the more difficult it is, the more highly it is regarded"。

4. 酸是一种化合物，它在溶于水时具有强烈的气味，它对金属具有腐蚀的作用，并且它具有把某些蓝色植物染料变红的能力。

Acids are chemical compounds that, in water solution, have a sharp taste, a corrosive action on metals, and the ability to turn certain blue vegetable dyes red.

写作法则提炼：中文表达"酸是一种化合物，它在溶于水时具有一种强烈的气味，它对金属具有一种腐蚀的作用，并且它具有把某些蓝色植物染料变红的能力"；英文表达"酸是化合物 that，进入水溶解作用，具有一种强烈的味道，一种腐蚀的作用对于金属，并且这种能力去转变某些蓝色植物染料红色的"，完全转换"Acids are chemical compounds that, in water solution, have a sharp taste, a corrosive action on metals, and the ability to turn certain blue vegetable dyes red"。

重点词汇列表

社会问题重点词汇

traditional virtue	传统美德
implement	贯彻，实施
collapse	崩溃，瓦解
phenomenon	现象
initial socialist market economy system	
	社会主义初级阶段的市场经济体制
planned economy system	计划经济体制
environmental pollution	环境污染
energy crisis	能源危机
Commercialism	商业主义
westernization	西方化，欧美化
erode	侵蚀，腐蚀
spiritual values	精神价值观
degenerate	退化，堕落
essence	精华
dross	糟粕
Confucianism	孔子学说，儒教，儒家（学说）
Buddhism	佛教
Taoism	道教，道家的学说
inherit	继承

101

prosper	昌盛，繁荣
communication	交流，沟通
cooperation	合作，协作
penetration	穿过，渗透
Internet Age	网络时代
blog	网络博客
Internet cafes	网吧
juvenile	青少年，少年
teenager	青少年(13 至 19 岁的人)
netizen	网民，网虫
online entertainment	在线娱乐
globalization	全球化
youngster	年青人，少年
cyberspace	网际空间，电脑空间
browsing Web pages	浏览网页
playing online games	玩网络游戏
downloading music	下载音乐
Internet "opium"	网络鸦片
demon world	魔兽世界
Internet Addiction Disorder	网迷症
criticism	批评，批判
inheritance	继承；继承物，遗产
traditional culture	传统文化
Filial Piety	孝道，孝顺，孝心
Humaneness	仁慈，仁道，仁爱

重点词汇列表

Confucian Tradition	儒家传统
energy conservation	能源节约
development	发展
prosperity	繁荣
stability	稳定
Notwithstanding	尽管，虽然
spiritual civilization	精神文明
material civilization	物质文明
state legislation	国家立法
social policy	社会政策
the World Trade Organization(WTO)	世界贸易组织
the 29th Olympic Games in 2008	2008 年第 29 届奥运会
the responsibilities and obligations	责任和义务
thrift	节俭，节约
honesty	诚实，正直
affection	亲情，情感
courtesy	谦恭有礼
loyalty	忠诚，忠实，忠贞
socialist modernization	社会主义现代化
energy-saving	能源节省
sustainable development	可持续发展
the national economy and the people's livelihood	国计民生
ecosystem	生态系统

global warming	全球变暖
renewable sources	可再生能源
the global ecological imbalance	全球生态失衡
cocaine or heroin addiction	可卡因或海洛因上瘾
HIV	艾滋病病毒
AIDS	艾滋病
Family Violence	家庭暴力
central government	中央政府
reemployment	再就业
Laid-Off Workers	下岗工人
social security fund	社会保障基金
the Minimum Living Standard Scheme	最低生活保障方案
counterfeits and unqualified products	假冒伪劣产品
intellectual property	知识产权
Trademark Law	商标法
the Copyright Law	版权法
Piracy	非法盗印，侵犯版权

人生哲理重点词汇

a philosophic theory	人生哲理
Huxley Thomas Henry	
	赫胥黎，托马斯·亨利(英国生理学家， 曾获 1963 年诺贝尔生理学 – 医学奖)
Einstein Albert	
	爱因斯坦·阿尔贝特(德裔美国理论 物理学家，曾获 1921 年诺贝尔奖)
realist	现实主义者
pessimist	悲观论者，悲观主义者
optimist	乐观主义者
enlightenment	启迪，启发
refinement	提炼，精炼
excel at	擅长于
ponder over	沉思，深思
Newton Sir Isaac	
	牛顿·艾萨克(英国数学家、科学家)
creative thinking	创造性思维
controversial factors	有争议的因素
contribute to	有助于，促成
diligence and frugality	勤俭节约
enthusiasm and optimism	热情而乐观
the Nobel Prize	诺贝尔奖
frustration	挫折，受挫

perseverance	百折不挠，坚定不移
favorable circumstances	顺境
adverse circumstances	逆境
cooperation	合作
learnedness and curiosity	博学而好问
illumination	照明，发光

Edison Thomas Alva

爱迪生·托马斯·阿尔瓦(美国发明家，有一千多项发明专利权)

Beethoven Ludwig van

贝多芬·路德维希·凡(德国作曲家)

Louis Pasteur

巴斯德·路易(法国化学家、细菌学家)

perspiration	汗液，汗水
inspiration	灵感，启发
Genius	天才
philosopher	哲学家
agonize	使极度痛苦，折磨
exhaust	使精疲力尽
intent	意图，目的，计划
disturb	打乱，扰乱
fatigue	使疲劳，使疲乏

后　记
——英文"写法"培养方法论

一、字、词与句子

一门语言的最基本单位是字和词。把不同的字和词组合起来就是句子。不同语言在记录或表达事物的时候，组合字和词的习惯不同，从而就有了"句式"的概念。汉文有汉文的句式，英文有英文的句式。要会书写一门语言，首先是能够书写字和词，然后是能够熟练运用这门语言组合字和词的习惯，或曰规则，也就是特有的种种句式。

二、语法、写法与读法

现在的英语写作教学大多是围绕语法教学展开。这是很不恰当的。语法很广，是整个语言使用的基本法则。写作必定要遵循这些"基本法则"，但遵循的同时也是要超越的。若没有超越的话，就没有"文采"可言，全天下的文章都是千篇一律了。写作有写作的法则，即写法。写法没有语法那么呆板，讲究的是优美。定语从句按照语法的要求必须要有关系代词，但习惯的写法很多时候是把关系代词省略的。并列句中前后相同的动词，按照语法来讲，是不省略的，但在写作中往往是把并列句中的相同动词省略的，这样看上去会更优美一点。对于外国的语言学习者，这些"省略"等的写法如果不知道的话，就是语法学的多么好的学习者，也不一定能读懂纯正的、优美的英文文章。所以，写法和读法是相通的。

三、写法的提炼与模仿

大文豪们的写作水平并不是练出来的，而是大量读书模仿出来的。所以，笔者主张写作的提高是在拥有大量的词汇基础之上，去模仿那些好的写法进行书面的表达。